GET IT TOGETHER!
WITH SARAH'S SCRIBBLES

16-MONTH
WEEKLY/MONTHLY
PLANNER
SEPTEMBER 2018-
DECEMBER 2019

SARAH ANDERSEN

Andrews McMeel
PUBLISHING®

Get It Together! with Sarah's Scribbles 16-Month Weekly/Monthly Planner © 2018 by Sarah Andersen. Printed in China. No part of this calendar may be used or reproduced in any manner whatsoever without written permission except in the case of reprints in the context of reviews. For information write Andrews McMeel Publishing, a division of Andrews McMeel Universal, 1130 Walnut Street, Kansas City, Missouri 64106.

ISBN-13: 978-1-4494-9406-3
www.gocomics.com/sarahs-scribbles
www.andrewsmcmeel.com

Every effort has been made to ensure the accuracy of listed holiday dates, however, some may have changed after publication for official or cultural reasons.

2019

JANUARY

S	M	T	W	T	F	S
		1	2	3	4	5
6	7	8	9	10	11	12
13	14	15	16	17	18	19
20	21	22	23	24	25	26
27	28	29	30	31		

FEBRUARY

S	M	T	W	T	F	S
					1	2
3	4	5	6	7	8	9
10	11	12	13	14	15	16
17	18	19	20	21	22	23
24	25	26	27	28		

MARCH

S	M	T	W	T	F	S
					1	2
3	4	5	6	7	8	9
10	11	12	13	14	15	16
17	18	19	20	21	22	23
24	25	26	27	28	29	30
31						

APRIL

S	M	T	W	T	F	S
	1	2	3	4	5	6
7	8	9	10	11	12	13
14	15	16	17	18	19	20
21	22	23	24	25	26	27
28	29	30				

MAY

S	M	T	W	T	F	S
			1	2	3	4
5	6	7	8	9	10	11
12	13	14	15	16	17	18
19	20	21	22	23	24	25
26	27	28	29	30	31	

JUNE

S	M	T	W	T	F	S
						1
2	3	4	5	6	7	8
9	10	11	12	13	14	15
16	17	18	19	20	21	22
23	24	25	26	27	28	29
30						

JULY

S	M	T	W	T	F	S
	1	2	3	4	5	6
7	8	9	10	11	12	13
14	15	16	17	18	19	20
21	22	23	24	25	26	27
28	29	30	31			

AUGUST

S	M	T	W	T	F	S
				1	2	3
4	5	6	7	8	9	10
11	12	13	14	15	16	17
18	19	20	21	22	23	24
25	26	27	28	29	30	31

SEPTEMBER

S	M	T	W	T	F	S
1	2	3	4	5	6	7
8	9	10	11	12	13	14
15	16	17	18	19	20	21
22	23	24	25	26	27	28
29	30					

OCTOBER

S	M	T	W	T	F	S
		1	2	3	4	5
6	7	8	9	10	11	12
13	14	15	16	17	18	19
20	21	22	23	24	25	26
27	28	29	30	31		

NOVEMBER

S	M	T	W	T	F	S
					1	2
3	4	5	6	7	8	9
10	11	12	13	14	15	16
17	18	19	20	21	22	23
24	25	26	27	28	29	30

DECEMBER

S	M	T	W	T	F	S
1	2	3	4	5	6	7
8	9	10	11	12	13	14
15	16	17	18	19	20	21
22	23	24	25	26	27	28
29	30	31				

SEPTEMBER 2018

SUN	MON	TUES	WED	THUR	FRI	SAT
NOTES AND STUFF						1
2 FATHER'S DAY (AUSTRALIA, NZ)	3 LABOR DAY (USA, CANADA)	4	5	6	7	8
9	10 ROSH HASHANAH*	11 ROSH HASHANAH ENDS	12	13	14	15
16	17	18	19 YOM KIPPUR*	20	21 U.N. INTERNATIONAL DAY OF PEACE	22
23	24 QUEEN'S BIRTHDAY (AUSTRALIA–WA)	25	26	27	28	29
30						

*BEGINS AT SUNDOWN THE PREVIOUS DAY

OCTOBER 2018

SUN	MON	TUES	WED	THUR	FRI	SAT
	1 LABOUR DAY (AUSTRALIA – ACT, SA, NSW) QUEEN'S BIRTHDAY (AUSTRALIA – QLD)	2	3	4	5	6
7	8 COLUMBUS DAY (USA) THANKSGIVING (CANADA)	9	10	11	12	13
14	15	16	17	18	19	20
21	22 LABOUR DAY (NZ)	23	24 UNITED NATIONS DAY	25	26	27
28	29 BANK HOLIDAY (IRELAND)	30	31 HALLOWEEN	NOTES AND STUFF		

NOVEMBER 2018

SUN	MON	TUES	WED	THUR	FRI	SAT
NOTES AND STUFF				1	2	3
4	5	6 ELECTION DAY (USA)	7	8	9	10
11 VETERANS' DAY (USA) REMEMBRANCE DAY (CANADA, IRELAND, UK)	12	13	14	15	16	17
18	19	20	21	22 THANKSGIVING (USA)	23	24
25	26	27	28	29	30 ST. ANDREW'S DAY (UK)	

DECEMBER 2018

SUN	MON	TUES	WED	THUR	FRI	SAT
NOTES AND STUFF .... *BEGINS AT SUNDOWN THE PREVIOUS DAY						1
2	3 HANUKKAH*	4	5	6	7	8
9	10 HANUKKAH ENDS HUMAN RIGHTS DAY	11	12	13	14	15
16	17	18	19	20	21	22
23	24 CHRISTMAS EVE	25 CHRISTMAS DAY	26 KWANZAA BEGINS (USA) BOXING DAY (CANADA, NZ, UK, AUSTRALIA – EXCEPT SA) ST. STEPHEN'S DAY (IRELAND) PROCLAMATION DAY (AUSTRALIA – SA)	27	28	29
30	31					

JANUARY 2019

SUN	MON	TUES	WED	THUR	FRI	SAT
		1 NEW YEAR'S DAY KWANZAA ENDS (USA)	2 NEW YEAR'S DAY (OBSERVED) (NZ) BANK HOLIDAY (UK – SCOTLAND)	3	4	5
6	7	8	9	10	11	12
13	14	15	16	17	18	19
20	21 MARTIN LUTHER KING JR. DAY (USA)	22	23	24	25	26 AUSTRALIA DAY
27	28 AUSTRALIA DAY (OBSERVED)	29	30	31	NOTES AND STUFF	

FEBRUARY 2019

SUN	MON	TUES	WED	THUR	FRI	SAT
NOTES AND STUFF					1	2
3	4	5	6	7	8	9
10	11	12	13 WAITANGI DAY (NZ)	14	15	16
17	18	19	20	21 ST. VALENTINE'S DAY	22	23
24	25 PRESIDENTS' DAY (USA)	26	27	28		

MARCH 2019

SUN	MON	TUES	WED	THUR	FRI	SAT
NOTES AND STUFF .... *BEGINS AT SUNDOWN THE PREVIOUS DAY					**1** ST. DAVID'S DAY (UK)	**2**
3	**4** LABOUR DAY (AUSTRALIA – WA)	**5**	**6** ASH WEDNESDAY	**7**	**8** INTERNATIONAL WOMEN'S DAY	**9**
10	**11** EIGHT HOURS DAY (AUSTRALIA – TAS) CANBERRA DAY (AUSTRALIA – ACT) LABOUR DAY (AUSTRALIA – VIC) COMMONWEALTH DAY (AUSTRALIA, CANADA, NZ, UK)	**12**	**13**	**14**	**15**	**16**
17 ST. PATRICK'S DAY	**18**	**19**	**20**	**21** PURIM*	**22**	**23**
24	**25**	**26**	**27**	**28**	**29**	**30**
31 MOTHERING SUNDAY (IRELAND, UK)						

APRIL 2019

SUN	MON	TUES	WED	THUR	FRI	SAT
	1	2	3	4	5	6
7	8	9	10	11	12	13
14 PALM SUNDAY	15	16	17	18	19 GOOD FRIDAY (WESTERN)	20 PASSOVER* EASTER SATURDAY (AUSTRALIA – EXCEPT TAS, WA)
21 EASTER (WESTERN)	22 EASTER MONDAY (AUSTRALIA, CANADA, IRELAND, NZ, UK – EXCEPT SCOTLAND) EARTH DAY	23 ST. GEORGE'S DAY (UK)	24	25 ANZAC DAY (NZ, AUSTRALIA)	26 HOLY FRIDAY (ORTHODOX)	27 PASSOVER ENDS
28 EASTER (ORTHODOX)	29	30				

NOTES AND STUFF

....

....

....

....

....

*BEGINS AT SUNDOWN THE PREVIOUS DAY

MAY 2019

SUN	MON	TUES	WED	THUR	FRI	SAT
NOTES AND STUFF ·· ·· ·· ·· ··			1	2	3	4
5 RAMADAN	6 MAY DAY (AUSTRALIA – NT) LABOUR DAY (AUSTRALIA – QLD) EARLY MAY BANK HOLIDAY (IRELAND, UK)	7	8	9	10	11
12 MOTHER'S DAY (USA, AUSTRALIA, CANADA, NZ)	13	14	15	16	17	18 ARMED FORCES DAY (USA)
19	20 VICTORIA DAY (CANADA)	21	22	23	24	25
26	27 MEMORIAL DAY (USA) SPRING BANK HOLIDAY (UK)	28	29	30	31	

JUNE 2019

SUN	MON	TUES	WED	THUR	FRI	SAT
NOTES AND STUFF						1
2	3 QUEEN'S BIRTHDAY (NZ) WESTERN AUSTRALIA DAY SPRING BANK HOLIDAY (IRELAND)	4 EID AL-FITR	5	6	7	8
9	10 QUEEN'S BIRTHDAY (AUSTRALIA – EXCEPT QLD, WA)	11	12	13	14 FLAG DAY (USA)	15
16 FATHER'S DAY (USA, CANADA, IRELAND, UK)	17	18	19	20	21	22
23	24	25	26	27	28	29
30						

JULY 2019

SUN	MON	TUES	WED	THUR	FRI	SAT
	1 CANADA DAY	2	3	4 INDEPENDENCE DAY (USA)	5	6
7	8	9	10	11	12	13
14	15	16	17	18	19	20
21	22	23	24	25	26	27
28	29	30	31	NOTES AND STUFF		

AUGUST 2019

SUN	MON	TUES	WED	THUR	FRI	SAT
NOTES AND STUFF				1	2	3
4	5 SUMMER BANK HOLIDAY (IRELAND, UK – SCOTLAND, AUSTRALIA – NSW) PICNIC DAY (AUSTRALIA – NT)	6	7	8	9	10
11 EID AL-ADHA	12	13	14	15	16	17
18	19	20	21	22	23	24
25	26 SUMMER BANK HOLIDAY (UK – EXCEPT SCOTLAND)	27	28	29	30	31

SEPTEMBER 2019

SUN	MON	TUES	WED	THUR	FRI	SAT
1 FATHER'S DAY (AUSTRALIA, NZ)	2 LABOR DAY (USA, CANADA)	3	4	5	6	7
8	9	10	11	12	13	14
15	16	17	18	19	20	21 U.N. INTERNATIONAL DAY OF PEACE
22	23	24	25	26	27	28
29	30 ROSH HASHANAH* QUEEN'S BIRTHDAY (AUSTRALIA – WA)	NOTES AND STUFF .... *BEGINS AT SUNDOWN THE PREVIOUS DAY				

OCTOBER 2019

SUN	MON	TUES	WED	THUR	FRI	SAT
		1 ROSH HASHANAH ENDS	2	3	4	5
6	7 LABOUR DAY (AUSTRALIA – ACT, SA, NSW) QUEEN'S BIRTHDAY (AUSTRALIA – QLD)	8	9 YOM KIPPUR*	10	11	12
13	14 COLUMBUS DAY (USA) THANKSGIVING (CANADA)	15	16	17	18	19
20	21	22	23	24 UNITED NATIONS DAY	25	26
27	28 LABOUR DAY (NZ) BANK HOLIDAY (IRELAND)	29	30	31 HALLOWEEN	NOTES AND STUFF .... *BEGINS AT SUNDOWN THE PREVIOUS DAY	

NOVEMBER 2019

SUN	MON	TUES	WED	THUR	FRI	SAT
NOTES AND STUFF					1	2
3	4	5 ELECTION DAY (USA)	6	7	8	9
10	11 VETERANS' DAY (USA) REMEMBRANCE DAY (CANADA, IRELAND, UK)	12	13	14	15	16
17	18	19	20	21	22	23
24	25	26	27	28 THANKSGIVING (USA)	29	30 ST. ANDREW'S DAY (UK)

DECEMBER 2019

SUN	MON	TUES	WED	THUR	FRI	SAT
1	2	3	4	5	6	7
8	9	10 HUMAN RIGHTS DAY	11	12	13	14
15	16	17	18	19	20	21
22	23 HANUKKAH*	24 CHRISTMAS EVE	25 CHRISTMAS DAY	26 KWANZAA BEGINS (USA) BOXING DAY (CANADA, NZ, UK, AUSTRALIA – EXCEPT SA) ST. STEPHEN'S DAY (IRELAND) PROCLAMATION DAY (AUSTRALIA – SA)	27	28
29	30 HANUKKAH ENDS	31				

NOTES AND STUFF

*BEGINS AT SUNDOWN THE PREVIOUS DAY

AUG-SEP

APPOINTMENTS/MISC

STUFF TO DO

27 MONDAY
SUMMER BANK HOLIDAY (UK – EXCEPT SCOTLAND)

28 TUESDAY

29 WEDNESDAY

30 THURSDAY

31 FRIDAY

1 SATURDAY

2 SUNDAY
FATHER'S DAY (AUSTRALIA, NZ)

MY ABILITIES

INTELLIGENCE

Pretty good!

MEMORY

Also good!

CREATIVITY

Good too!

TIME MANAGEMENT

HOP

WHERE IS IT

NOTES AND STUFF

....

....

....

....

....

....

AUGUST 2018

S	M	T	W	T	F	S
			1	2	3	4
5	6	7	8	9	10	11
12	13	14	15	16	17	18
19	20	21	22	23	24	25
26	27	28	29	30	31	

SEPTEMBER 2018

S	M	T	W	T	F	S
						1
2	3	4	5	6	7	8
9	10	11	12	13	14	15
16	17	18	19	20	21	22
23	24	25	26	27	28	29
30						

SEPTEMBER

APPOINTMENTS/MISC

STUFF TO DO

3 MONDAY

LABOR DAY (USA, CANADA)

4 TUESDAY

5 WEDNESDAY

6 THURSDAY

7 FRIDAY

8 SATURDAY

9 SUNDAY

MY SOCIAL LIFE

BUG.

...No problem!

VRRR

NOTES AND STUFF

SEPTEMBER 2018
S M T W T F S
                1
2 3 4 5 6 7 8
9 10 11 12 13 14 15
16 17 18 19 20 21 22
23 24 25 26 27 28 29
30

SEPTEMBER

10 MONDAY
ROSH HASHANAH*

11 TUESDAY
ROSH HASHANAH ENDS

12 WEDNESDAY

13 THURSDAY

14 FRIDAY

15 SATURDAY

16 SUNDAY

*Begins at sundown the previous d

NOTEBOOKS:
EXPECTATION

Wow, Gramma!

What an intricate, beautiful record of your life.

REALITY

WHAT THE-

You have hundreds of notebooks with only like three pages filled.

Yes... Notebooks were my greatest weakness.

NOTES AND STUFF

SEPTEMBER 2018

S	M	T	W	T	F	S
						1
2	3	4	5	6	7	8
9	10	11	12	13	14	15
16	17	18	19	20	21	22
23	24	25	26	27	28	29
30						

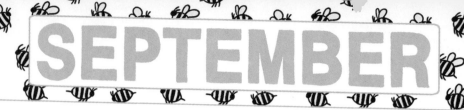
SEPTEMBER

	APPOINTMENTS/MISC	STUFF TO DO

17 MONDAY

18 TUESDAY

19 WEDNESDAY

YOM KIPPUR*

20 THURSDAY

21 FRIDAY

U.N. INTERNATIONAL DAY OF PEACE

22 SATURDAY

23 SUNDAY

*Begins at sundown the previous day

MY SOCIAL LIFE

WHY AM I HAVING TROUBLE SLEEPING?

Anxiety.

WHY DOES MY STOMACH ALWAYS HURT?

Anxiety.

WHY DOES MY CHEST FEEL TIGHT?

Anxiety.

WHAT could it BE??

IT IS ANXIETY

NOTES AND STUFF

SEPTEMBER 2018
S M T W T F S
                            1
2 3 4 5 6 7 8
9 10 11 12 13 14 15
16 17 18 19 20 21 22
23 24 25 26 27 28 29
30

SEPTEMBER

	APPOINTMENTS/MISC	STUFF TO DO
24 MONDAY		
QUEEN'S BIRTHDAY (AUSTRALIA – WA)		
25 TUESDAY		
26 WEDNESDAY		
27 THURSDAY		
28 FRIDAY		
29 SATURDAY		
30 SUNDAY		

MY SOCIAL LIFE

ME:

ME, IF MY SECRET INNER STRENGTH WAS PHYSICAL:

NOTES AND STUFF

SEPTEMBER 2018
S M T W T F S
                    1
2 3 4 5 6 7 8
9 10 11 12 13 14 15
16 17 18 19 20 21 22
23 24 25 26 27 28 29
30

OCTOBER

1 MONDAY

LABOUR DAY (AUSTRALIA – ACT, SA, NSW)
QUEEN'S BIRTHDAY (AUSTRALIA – QLD)

2 TUESDAY

3 WEDNESDAY

4 THURSDAY

5 FRIDAY

6 SATURDAY

7 SUNDAY

MY SOCIAL LIFE

NOTES AND STUFF

OCTOBER 2018
S M T W T F S
1 2 3 4 5 6
7 8 9 10 11 12 13
14 15 16 17 18 19 20
21 22 23 24 25 26 27
28 29 30 31

OCTOBER

8 MONDAY

COLUMBUS DAY (USA)
THANKSGIVING (CANADA)

9 TUESDAY

10 WEDNESDAY

11 THURSDAY

12 FRIDAY

13 SATURDAY

14 SUNDAY

SOCIETAL MYTH

Artist + sadness = Great art

THE REALITY

Artist + sadness = Uninspired, sad artist

TRUTH

Content, happy artist = Artist happily working

NOTES AND STUFF

....
....
....
....
....
....
....

OCTOBER 2018

S	M	T	W	T	F	S
	1	2	3	4	5	6
7	8	9	10	11	12	13
14	15	16	17	18	19	20
21	22	23	24	25	26	27
28	29	30	31			

OCTOBER

	APPOINTMENTS/MISC	STUFF TO DO
15 MONDAY		
16 TUESDAY		
17 WEDNESDAY		
18 THURSDAY		
19 FRIDAY		
20 SATURDAY		
21 SUNDAY		

SPENDING A DAY OFFLINE: 2010

Oh...I guess I didn't check Facebook today.

TODAY

· · · · · · · · · THINGS · · · ·

· · · · ·

Rip

· · · · ARE REAL...

NOTES AND STUFF

....

....

....

OCTOBER 2018

S	M	T	W	T	F	S
	1	2	3	4	5	6
7	8	9	10	11	12	13
14	15	16	17	18	19	20
21	22	23	24	25	26	27
28	29	30	31			

OCTOBER

22 MONDAY

LABOUR DAY (NZ)

23 TUESDAY

24 WEDNESDAY

UNITED NATIONS DAY

25 THURSDAY

26 FRIDAY

27 SATURDAY

28 SUNDAY

NOTES AND STUFF

....
....
....
....
....
....

OCTOBER 2018
S M T W T F S
      1 2 3 4 5 6
7 8 9 10 11 12 13
14 15 16 17 18 19 20
21 22 23 24 25 26 27
28 29 30 31

OCT-NOV

APPOINTMENTS/MISC

STUFF TO DO

29 MONDAY

BANK HOLIDAY (IRELAND)

30 TUESDAY

31 WEDNESDAY

HALLOWEEN

1 THURSDAY

2 FRIDAY

3 SATURDAY

4 SUNDAY

MY SOCIAL LIFE

NOTES AND STUFF

....
....
....
....
....
....
....
....
....
....
....

OCTOBER 2018

S	M	T	W	T	F	S
	1	2	3	4	5	6
7	8	9	10	11	12	13
14	15	16	17	18	19	20
21	22	23	24	25	26	27
28	29	30	31			

NOVEMBER 2018

S	M	T	W	T	F	S
				1	2	3
4	5	6	7	8	9	10
11	12	13	14	15	16	17
18	19	20	21	22	23	24
25	26	27	28	29	30	

NOVEMBER

APPOINTMENTS/MISC

STUFF TO DO

5 MONDAY

6 TUESDAY

ELECTION DAY (USA)

7 WEDNESDAY

8 THURSDAY

9 FRIDAY

10 SATURDAY

11 SUNDAY

VETERANS' DAY (USA)
REMEMBRANCE DAY (CANADA, IRELAND, UK)

MY SOCIAL LIFE

NOTES AND STUFF

....
....
....
....
....
....

NOVEMBER 2018

S	M	T	W	T	F	S
				1	2	3
4	5	6	7	8	9	10
11	12	13	14	15	16	17
18	19	20	21	22	23	24
25	26	27	28	29	30	

NOVEMBER

12	MONDAY
13	TUESDAY
14	WEDNESDAY
15	THURSDAY
16	FRIDAY
17	SATURDAY
18	SUNDAY

MY SOCIAL LIFE

NOTES AND STUFF

....
....
....
....
....
....

NOVEMBER 2018
S M T W T F S
          1 2 3
4 5 6 7 8 9 10
11 12 13 14 15 16 17
18 19 20 21 22 23 24
25 26 27 28 29 30

NOVEMBER

19 MONDAY

20 TUESDAY

21 WEDNESDAY

22 THURSDAY

THANKSGIVING (USA)

23 FRIDAY

24 SATURDAY

25 SUNDAY

NOTES AND STUFF

NOVEMBER 2018

S	M	T	W	T	F	S
				1	2	3
4	5	6	7	8	9	10
11	12	13	14	15	16	17
18	19	20	21	22	23	24
25	26	27	28	29	30	

NOV-DEC

APPOINTMENTS/MISC

STUFF TO DO

26 MONDAY

27 TUESDAY

28 WEDNESDAY

29 THURSDAY

30 FRIDAY

ST. ANDREW'S DAY (UK)

1 SATURDAY

2 SUNDAY

MY SOCIAL LIFE

NOTES AND STUFF

NOVEMBER 2018
S M T W T F S
            1 2 3
4 5 6 7 8 9 10
11 12 13 14 15 16 17
18 19 20 21 22 23 24
25 26 27 28 29 30

DECEMBER 2018
S M T W T F S
                  1
2 3 4 5 6 7 8
9 10 11 12 13 14 15
16 17 18 19 20 21 22
23 24 25 26 27 28 29
30 31

DECEMBER

	APPOINTMENTS/MISC	STUFF TO DO

3 MONDAY

HANUKKAH*

4 TUESDAY

5 WEDNESDAY

6 THURSDAY

7 FRIDAY

8 SATURDAY

9 SUNDAY

*Begins at sundown the previous day

BEFORE AND AFTER FAME: ACTORS

MUSICIANS

ARTISTS

NOTES AND STUFF

....

....

....

....

....

DECEMBER 2018

S	M	T	W	T	F	S
						1
2	3	4	5	6	7	8
9	10	11	12	13	14	15
16	17	18	19	20	21	22
23	24	25	26	27	28	29
30	31					

DECEMBER

10 MONDAY
HANUKKAH ENDS
HUMAN RIGHTS DAY

11 TUESDAY

12 WEDNESDAY

13 THURSDAY

14 FRIDAY

15 SATURDAY

16 SUNDAY

MY SOCIAL LIFE

....

....

....

....

....

....

"SYNCING"

Oh! Hey again!

Hey!

I've been seeing you around a lot lately!

We should try to meet up more often!

Totally!

Maybe sometime later this month?

LATER THAT MONTH

NOTES AND STUFF

....

....

....

....

....

....

....

DECEMBER 2018

S M T W T F S

            1

2 3 4 5 6 7 8

9 10 11 12 13 14 15

16 17 18 19 20 21 22

23 24 25 26 27 28 29

30 31

DECEMBER

17 MONDAY

18 TUESDAY

19 WEDNESDAY

20 THURSDAY

21 FRIDAY

22 SATURDAY

23 SUNDAY

MY SOCIAL LIFE

OLD CARTOONING

1) Draw comic

2) Turn it in

NEW CARTOONING

1) Draw comic

2) Turn it in

SUBMIT

3) Pray for sweet mercy from the comments section

NOTES AND STUFF

....
....
....
....
....
....

DECEMBER 2018
S M T W T F S
                    1
2 3 4 5 6 7 8
9 10 11 12 13 14 15
16 17 18 19 20 21 22
23 24 25 26 27 28 29
30 31

DECEMBER

APPOINTMENTS/MISC

STUFF TO DO

24 MONDAY

CHRISTMAS EVE

25 TUESDAY

CHRISTMAS DAY

26 WEDNESDAY

KWANZAA BEGINS (USA)
BOXING DAY (CANADA, NZ, UK, AUSTRALIA – EXCEPT SA)
ST. STEPHEN'S DAY (IRELAND)
PROCLAMATION DAY (AUSTRALIA – SA)

27 THURSDAY

28 FRIDAY

29 SATURDAY

30 SUNDAY

MY SOCIAL LIFE

....

....

....

....

....

....

TAKING CARE OF MYSELF

Eating healthy

Reasonable, productive work hours

Normal sleep schedule

NOTES AND STUFF

....

....

....

DECEMBER 2018

S M T W T F S
                    1
2 3 4 5 6 7 8
9 10 11 12 13 14 15
16 17 18 19 20 21 22
23 24 25 26 27 28 29
30 31

DEC-JAN

APPOINTMENTS/MISC

STUFF TO DO

31 MONDAY

1 TUESDAY

NEW YEAR'S DAY
KWANZAA ENDS (USA)

2 WEDNESDAY

NEW YEAR'S DAY (OBSERVED) (NZ)
BANK HOLIDAY (UK – SCOTLAND)

3 THURSDAY

4 FRIDAY

5 SATURDAY

6 SUNDAY

MY SOCIAL LIFE

GASP

DRAAAAAG

DRAAG

WHEEZE

NEW YEARS

YOU MADE IT!!!

NEW YEAR

NOTES AND STUFF

....

....

....

....

DECEMBER 2018
S M T W T F S

1
2 3 4 5 6 7 8
9 10 11 12 13 14 15
16 17 18 19 20 21 22
23 24 25 26 27 28 29
30 31

JANUARY 2019
S M T W T F S
1 2 3 4 5
6 7 8 9 10 11 12
13 14 15 16 17 18 19
20 21 22 23 24 25 26
27 28 29 30 31

JANUARY

APPOINTMENTS/MISC

STUFF TO DO

7 MONDAY

8 TUESDAY

9 WEDNESDAY

10 THURSDAY

11 FRIDAY

12 SATURDAY

13 SUNDAY

MY SOCIAL LIFE

NOTES AND STUFF

JANUARY 2019
S M T W T F S
1 2 3 4 5
6 7 8 9 10 11 12
13 14 15 16 17 18 19
20 21 22 23 24 25 26
27 28 29 30 31

JANUARY

APPOINTMENTS/MISC	STUFF TO DO

14 MONDAY

15 TUESDAY

16 WEDNESDAY

17 THURSDAY

18 FRIDAY

19 SATURDAY

20 SUNDAY

MY SOCIAL LIFE

NOTES AND STUFF

....
....
....
....

JANUARY 2019
S M T W T F S
1 2 3 4 5
6 7 8 9 10 11 12
13 14 15 16 17 18 19
20 21 22 23 24 25 26
27 28 29 30 31

....
....

JANUARY

APPOINTMENTS/MISC

STUFF TO DO

21 MONDAY

MARTIN LUTHER KING JR. DAY (USA)

22 TUESDAY

23 WEDNESDAY

24 THURSDAY

25 FRIDAY

26 SATURDAY

AUSTRALIA DAY

27 SUNDAY

NOTES AND STUFF

....
....
....
....

JANUARY 2019

S	M	T	W	T	F	S
		1	2	3	4	5
6	7	8	9	10	11	12
13	14	15	16	17	18	19
20	21	22	23	24	25	26
27	28	29	30	31		

JAN-FEB

28 MONDAY
AUSTRALIA DAY (OBSERVED)

29 TUESDAY

30 WEDNESDAY

31 THURSDAY

1 FRIDAY

2 SATURDAY

3 SUNDAY

MY SOCIAL LIFE

....

....

....

....

....

....

....

NOTES AND STUFF

....

....

....

....

....

....

....

....

....

....

....

....

....

....

....

JANUARY 2019

S	M	T	W	T	F	S
		1	2	3	4	5
6	7	8	9	10	11	12
13	14	15	16	17	18	19
20	21	22	23	24	25	26
27	28	29	30	31		

FEBRUARY 2019

S	M	T	W	T	F	S
					1	2
3	4	5	6	7	8	9
10	11	12	13	14	15	16
17	18	19	20	21	22	23
24	25	26	27	28		

FEBRUARY

	APPOINTMENTS/MISC	STUFF TO DO
4 MONDAY		
5 TUESDAY		
6 WEDNESDAY WAITANGI DAY (NZ)		
7 THURSDAY		
8 FRIDAY		
9 SATURDAY		
10 SUNDAY		

NOTES AND STUFF

....

....

....

....

FEBRUARY 2019

S M T W T F S

         1 2
3 4 5 6 7 8 9
10 11 12 13 14 15 16
17 18 19 20 21 22 23
24 25 26 27 28

FEBRUARY

	APPOINTMENTS/MISC	STUFF TO DO
11 MONDAY		
12 TUESDAY		
13 WEDNESDAY		
14 THURSDAY ST. VALENTINE'S DAY		
15 FRIDAY		
16 SATURDAY		
17 SUNDAY		

NOTES AND STUFF

FEBRUARY 2019

S	M	T	W	T	F	S
					1	2
3	4	5	6	7	8	9
10	11	12	13	14	15	16
17	18	19	20	21	22	23
24	25	26	27	28		

FEBRUARY

18 MONDAY

PRESIDENTS' DAY (USA)

19 TUESDAY

20 WEDNESDAY

21 THURSDAY

22 FRIDAY

23 SATURDAY

24 SUNDAY

NOTES AND STUFF

....

....

....

....

....

....

....

FEBRUARY 2019

S M T W T F S

1 2

3 4 5 6 7 8 9

10 11 12 13 14 15 16

17 18 19 20 21 22 23

24 25 26 27 28

	APPOINTMENTS/MISC	STUFF TO DO
25 MONDAY		
26 TUESDAY		
27 WEDNESDAY		
28 THURSDAY		
1 FRIDAY ST. DAVID'S DAY (UK)		
2 SATURDAY		
3 SUNDAY		

NOTES AND STUFF

FEBRUARY 2019
S M T W T F S
| | | | | | 1 2
3 4 5 6 7 8 9
10 11 12 13 14 15 16
17 18 19 20 21 22 23
24 25 26 27 28

MARCH 2019
S M T W T F S
| | | | | | 1 2
3 4 5 6 7 8 9
10 11 12 13 14 15 16
17 18 19 20 21 22 23
24 25 26 27 28 29 30
31

MARCH

4 MONDAY

LABOUR DAY (AUSTRALIA – WA)

5 TUESDAY

6 WEDNESDAY

ASH WEDNESDAY

7 THURSDAY

8 FRIDAY

INTERNATIONAL WOMEN'S DAY

9 SATURDAY

10 SUNDAY

NOTES AND STUFF

....
....
....
....
....

MARCH 2019

S	M	T	W	T	F	S
					1	2
3	4	5	6	7	8	9
10	11	12	13	14	15	16
17	18	19	20	21	22	23
24	25	26	27	28	29	30
31						

MARCH

APPOINTMENTS/MISC

STUFF TO DO

11 MONDAY

EIGHT HOURS DAY (AUSTRALIA – TAS)
CANBERRA DAY (AUSTRALIA – ACT)
LABOUR DAY (AUSTRALIA – VIC)
COMMONWEALTH DAY (AUSTRALIA, CANADA, NZ, UK)

12 TUESDAY

13 WEDNESDAY

14 THURSDAY

15 FRIDAY

16 SATURDAY

17 SUNDAY

ST. PATRICK'S DAY

MY SOCIAL LIFE

....

....

....

....

....

....

NOTES AND STUFF

....

....

....

....

....

....

....

....

MARCH 2019

S	M	T	W	T	F	S
					1	2
3	4	5	6	7	8	9
10	11	12	13	14	15	16
17	18	19	20	21	22	23
24	25	26	27	28	29	30
31						

MARCH

APPOINTMENTS/MISC

STUFF TO DO

18 MONDAY

19 TUESDAY

20 WEDNESDAY

21 THURSDAY

PURIM*

22 FRIDAY

23 SATURDAY

24 SUNDAY

MY SOCIAL LIFE

NOTES AND STUFF

....
....
....
....

MARCH 2019
S M T W T F S
       1 2
3 4 5 6 7 8 9
10 11 12 13 14 15 16
17 18 19 20 21 22 23
24 25 26 27 28 29 30
31

MARCH

APPOINTMENTS/MISC	STUFF TO DO

25 MONDAY

26 TUESDAY

27 WEDNESDAY

28 THURSDAY

29 FRIDAY

30 SATURDAY

31 SUNDAY

MOTHERING SUNDAY (IRELAND, UK)

MY SOCIAL LIFE

....

....

....

....

....

....

CLEANING TIPS

1) Donate clothes that don't fit

2) Clean out expired cosmetics

3) Get rid of old—

Do not, under any circumstances, get rid of old stuffed animals

NOTES AND STUFF

....

....

....

....

....

....

....

MARCH 2019

S	M	T	W	T	F	S
					1	2
3	4	5	6	7	8	9
10	11	12	13	14	15	16
17	18	19	20	21	22	23
24	25	26	27	28	29	30
31						

APRIL

	APPOINTMENTS/MISC	STUFF TO DO
1 MONDAY		
2 TUESDAY		
3 WEDNESDAY		
4 THURSDAY		
5 FRIDAY		
6 SATURDAY		
7 SUNDAY		

NOTES AND STUFF

APRIL 2019

S	M	T	W	T	F	S
	1	2	3	4	5	6
7	8	9	10	11	12	13
14	15	16	17	18	19	20
21	22	23	24	25	26	27
28	29	30				

APRIL

APPOINTMENTS/MISC

STUFF TO DO

8 MONDAY

9 TUESDAY

10 WEDNESDAY

11 THURSDAY

12 FRIDAY

13 SATURDAY

14 SUNDAY

PALM SUNDAY

LOGICAL PATH

OVER-THINKERS PATH

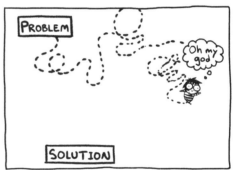

NOTES AND STUFF

....

....

....

....

....

APRIL 2019
S M T W T F S
1 2 3 4 5 6
7 8 9 10 11 12 13
14 15 16 17 18 19 20
21 22 23 24 25 26 27
28 29 30

APPOINTMENTS/MISC

STUFF TO DO

15 MONDAY

16 TUESDAY

17 WEDNESDAY

18 THURSDAY

19 FRIDAY

GOOD FRIDAY (WESTERN)

20 SATURDAY

PASSOVER*
EASTER SATURDAY (AUSTRALIA – EXCEPT TAS, WA)

21 SUNDAY

EASTER (WESTERN)

*Begins at sundown the previous day

HOW TO ENJOY A RAINY DAY

1) Find a cuddle buddy

2) A hot drink

3) A good movie

NETFLIX

4) A blanket pile

5) Enjoy being the coziest human ever.

NOTES AND STUFF

....

....

....

....

....

APRIL 2019
S M T W T F S
      1 2 3 4 5 6
7 8 9 10 11 12 13
14 15 16 17 18 19 20
21 22 23 24 25 26 27
28 29 30

APRIL

	APPOINTMENTS/MISC	STUFF TO DO

22 MONDAY

EASTER MONDAY (AUSTRALIA, CANADA, IRELAND, NZ, UK – EXCEPT SCOTLAND)
EARTH DAY

23 TUESDAY

ST. GEORGE'S DAY (UK)

24 WEDNESDAY

25 THURSDAY

ANZAC DAY (NZ, AUSTRALIA)

26 FRIDAY

HOLY FRIDAY (ORTHODOX)

27 SATURDAY

PASSOVER ENDS

28 SUNDAY

EASTER (ORTHODOX)

MY SOCIAL LIFE

CAT SHAPES

Round

Long

Curve

Loaf

DOG SHAPES

Dog

NOTES AND STUFF

....
....
....
....
....
....

APRIL 2019

S	M	T	W	T	F	S
	1	2	3	4	5	6
7	8	9	10	11	12	13
14	15	16	17	18	19	20
21	22	23	24	25	26	27
28	29	30				

APR-MAY

APPOINTMENTS/MISC

STUFF TO DO

29 MONDAY

30 TUESDAY

1 WEDNESDAY

2 THURSDAY

3 FRIDAY

4 SATURDAY

5 SUNDAY

RAMADAN

NOTES AND STUFF

....

....

....

....

....

....

....

....

....

APRIL 2019
S M T W T F S
       1 2 3 4 5 6
 7 8 9 10 11 12 13
14 15 16 17 18 19 20
21 22 23 24 25 26 27
28 29 30

MAY 2019
S M T W T F S
          1 2 3 4
 5 6 7 8 9 10 11
12 13 14 15 16 17 18
19 20 21 22 23 24 25
26 27 28 29 30 31

MAY

APPOINTMENTS/MISC

STUFF TO DO

6 MONDAY

MAY DAY (AUSTRALIA – NT)
LABOUR DAY (AUSTRALIA – QLD)
EARLY MAY BANK HOLIDAY (IRELAND, UK)

7 TUESDAY

8 WEDNESDAY

9 THURSDAY

10 FRIDAY

11 SATURDAY

12 SUNDAY

MOTHER'S DAY (USA, AUSTRALIA, CANADA, NZ)

NOTES AND STUFF
....
....
....
....

MAY 2019
S M T W T F S
          1 2 3 4
5 6 7 8 9 10 11
12 13 14 15 16 17 18
19 20 21 22 23 24 25
26 27 28 29 30 31

MAY

	APPOINTMENTS/MISC	STUFF TO DO
13 MONDAY		
14 TUESDAY		
15 WEDNESDAY		
16 THURSDAY		
17 FRIDAY		
18 SATURDAY ARMED FORCES DAY (USA)		
19 SUNDAY		

NOTES AND STUFF

....
....
....
....
....

MAY 2019

S	M	T	W	T	F	S
			1	2	3	4
5	6	7	8	9	10	11
12	13	14	15	16	17	18
19	20	21	22	23	24	25
26	27	28	29	30	31	

MAY

APPOINTMENTS/MISC

STUFF TO DO

20 MONDAY

VICTORIA DAY (CANADA)

21 TUESDAY

22 WEDNESDAY

23 THURSDAY

24 FRIDAY

25 SATURDAY

26 SUNDAY

NOTES AND STUFF

MAY 2019

S	M	T	W	T	F	S
			1	2	3	4
5	6	7	8	9	10	11
12	13	14	15	16	17	18
19	20	21	22	23	24	25
26	27	28	29	30	31	

MAY-JUN

APPOINTMENTS/MISC

STUFF TO DO

27 MONDAY

MEMORIAL DAY (USA)
SPRING BANK HOLIDAY (UK)

28 TUESDAY

29 WEDNESDAY

30 THURSDAY

31 FRIDAY

1 SATURDAY

2 SUNDAY

NOTES AND STUFF

....
....
....
....
....
....
....
....

MAY 2019
S M T W T F S
      1 2 3 4
5 6 7 8 9 10 11
12 13 14 15 16 17 18
19 20 21 22 23 24 25
26 27 28 29 30 31

JUNE 2019
S M T W T F S
            1
2 3 4 5 6 7 8
9 10 11 12 13 14 15
16 17 18 19 20 21 22
23 24 25 26 27 28 29
30

JUNE

3 MONDAY

QUEEN'S BIRTHDAY (NZ)
WESTERN AUSTRALIA DAY
SPRING BANK HOLIDAY (IRELAND)

4 TUESDAY

EID AL-FITR

5 WEDNESDAY

6 THURSDAY

7 FRIDAY

8 SATURDAY

9 SUNDAY

NOTES AND STUFF

....
....
....
....
....
....
....
....
....
....
....
....
....
....

JUNE 2019

S	M	T	W	T	F	S
						1
2	3	4	5	6	7	8
9	10	11	12	13	14	15
16	17	18	19	20	21	22
23	24	25	26	27	28	29
30						

JUNE

APPOINTMENTS/MISC

STUFF TO DO

10 MONDAY
QUEEN'S BIRTHDAY (AUSTRALIA – EXCEPT QLD, WA)

11 TUESDAY

12 WEDNESDAY

13 THURSDAY

14 FRIDAY
FLAG DAY (USA)

15 SATURDAY

16 SUNDAY
FATHER'S DAY (USA, CANADA, IRELAND, UK)

GREETING A DOG

NOTES AND STUFF

JUNE 2019

S	M	T	W	T	F	S
						1
2	3	4	5	6	7	8
9	10	11	12	13	14	15
16	17	18	19	20	21	22
23	24	25	26	27	28	29
30						

JUNE

17	MONDAY
18	TUESDAY
19	WEDNESDAY
20	THURSDAY
21	FRIDAY
22	SATURDAY
23	SUNDAY

NOTES AND STUFF

....
....
....
....
....
....
....
....
....

JUNE 2019
S M T W T F S
                    1
2 3 4 5 6 7 8
9 10 11 12 13 14 15
16 17 18 19 20 21 22
23 24 25 26 27 28 29
30

JUNE

	APPOINTMENTS/MISC	STUFF TO DO
24 MONDAY		
25 TUESDAY		
26 WEDNESDAY		
27 THURSDAY		
28 FRIDAY		
29 SATURDAY		
30 SUNDAY		

CHECKING THE NEWS:
MOST OF MY LIFE

Hm.

sip_

NOW

sip_

-SO MUCH INTERNAL
SCREAMING-

NOTES AND STUFF

....

....

....

....

....

....

....

JUNE 2019

S	M	T	W	T	F	S
						1
2	3	4	5	6	7	8
9	10	11	12	13	14	15
16	17	18	19	20	21	22
23	24	25	26	27	28	29
30						

JULY

APPOINTMENTS/MISC

STUFF TO DO

1 MONDAY
CANADA DAY

2 TUESDAY

3 WEDNESDAY

4 THURSDAY
INDEPENDENCE DAY (USA)

5 FRIDAY

6 SATURDAY

7 SUNDAY

SUMMER LOOKS!
MORNING

HAUTE

AFTERNOON
HOT

NOTES AND STUFF

....
....
....
....
....
....
....

JULY 2019
S	M	T	W	T	F	S
	1	2	3	4	5	6
7	8	9	10	11	12	13
14	15	16	17	18	19	20
21	22	23	24	25	26	27
28	29	30	31			

JULY

	APPOINTMENTS/MISC	STUFF TO DO
8 MONDAY		
9 TUESDAY		
10 WEDNESDAY		
11 THURSDAY		
12 FRIDAY		
13 SATURDAY		
14 SUNDAY		

MY SOCIAL LIFE

NOTES AND STUFF

....
....
....
....
....

JULY 2019
S M T W T F S
      1 2 3 4 5 6
7 8 9 10 11 12 13
14 15 16 17 18 19 20
21 22 23 24 25 26 27
28 29 30 31

JULY

APPOINTMENTS/MISC

STUFF TO DO

15	MONDAY
16	TUESDAY
17	WEDNESDAY
18	THURSDAY
19	FRIDAY
20	SATURDAY
21	SUNDAY

MY SOCIAL LIFE

NOTES AND STUFF

....
....
....
....
....
....
....
....
....
....
....
....
....
....
....
....
....
....
....
....

JULY 2019

S	M	T	W	T	F	S
	1	2	3	4	5	6
7	8	9	10	11	12	13
14	15	16	17	18	19	20
21	22	23	24	25	26	27
28	29	30	31			

JULY

APPOINTMENTS/MISC

STUFF TO DO

22 MONDAY

23 TUESDAY

24 WEDNESDAY

25 THURSDAY

26 FRIDAY

27 SATURDAY

28 SUNDAY

NOTES AND STUFF

....
....
....
....
....
....

JULY 2019
S M T W T F S
1 2 3 4 5 6
7 8 9 10 11 12 13
14 15 16 17 18 19 20
21 22 23 24 25 26 27
28 29 30 31

JUL-AUG

APPOINTMENTS/MISC	STUFF TO DO

29 MONDAY

30 TUESDAY

31 WEDNESDAY

1 THURSDAY

2 FRIDAY

3 SATURDAY

4 SUNDAY

MY SOCIAL LIFE

NOTES AND STUFF

....

....

....

....

....

....

....

JULY 2019
S M T W T F S
1 2 3 4 5 6
7 8 9 10 11 12 13
14 15 16 17 18 19 20
21 22 23 24 25 26 27
28 29 30 31

AUGUST 2019
S M T W T F S
1 2 3
4 5 6 7 8 9 10
11 12 13 14 15 16 17
18 19 20 21 22 23 24
25 26 27 28 29 30 31

AUGUST

APPOINTMENTS/MISC

STUFF TO DO

5 MONDAY

SUMMER BANK HOLIDAY
(IRELAND, UK – SCOTLAND, AUSTRALIA – NSW)
PICNIC DAY (AUSTRALIA – NT)

6 TUESDAY

7 WEDNESDAY

8 THURSDAY

9 FRIDAY

10 SATURDAY

11 SUNDAY

EID AL-ADHA

MOST PEOPLE

ME

NOTES AND STUFF

....

....

....

....

AUGUST 2019

S	M	T	W	T	F	S
				1	2	3
4	5	6	7	8	9	10
11	12	13	14	15	16	17
18	19	20	21	22	23	24
25	26	27	28	29	30	31

AUGUST

APPOINTMENTS/MISC

STUFF TO DO

12	MONDAY
13	TUESDAY
14	WEDNESDAY
15	THURSDAY
16	FRIDAY
17	SATURDAY
18	SUNDAY

MY SOCIAL LIFE

··

··

··

··

··

··

BANGS IN THE WINTER

BANGS IN THE SUMMER

NOTES AND STUFF

··
··
··
··
··
··
··
··
··
··
··
··
··
··
··
··
··
··
··
··
··

AUGUST 2019
S M T W T F S
            1 2 3
4 5 6 7 8 9 10
11 12 13 14 15 16 17
18 19 20 21 22 23 24
25 26 27 28 29 30 31

AUGUST

	APPOINTMENTS/MISC	STUFF TO DO
19 MONDAY		
20 TUESDAY		
21 WEDNESDAY		
22 THURSDAY		
23 FRIDAY		
24 SATURDAY		
25 SUNDAY		

NOTES AND STUFF

....
....
....
....
....
....

AUGUST 2019
S M T W T F S
            1 2 3
4 5 6 7 8 9 10
11 12 13 14 15 16 17
18 19 20 21 22 23 24
25 26 27 28 29 30 31

AUG-SEP

APPOINTMENTS/MISC

STUFF TO DO

26 MONDAY

SUMMER BANK HOLIDAY (UK – EXCEPT SCOTLAND)

27 TUESDAY

28 WEDNESDAY

29 THURSDAY

30 FRIDAY

31 SATURDAY

1 SUNDAY

FATHER'S DAY (AUSTRALIA, NZ)

....

....

....

....

....

....

....

"LIFE BEGINS AT THE END OF YOUR COMFORT ZONE"

FLICK

DING

PROGRESS

NOTES AND STUFF

....

....

....

....

AUGUST 2019
S M T W T F S
          1 2 3
4 5 6 7 8 9 10
11 12 13 14 15 16 17
18 19 20 21 22 23 24
25 26 27 28 29 30 31

SEPTEMBER 2019
S M T W T F S
1 2 3 4 5 6 7
8 9 10 11 12 13 14
15 16 17 18 19 20 21
22 23 24 25 26 27 28
29 30

SEPTEMBER

	APPOINTMENTS/MISC	STUFF TO DO

2 MONDAY

LABOR DAY (USA, CANADA)

3 TUESDAY

4 WEDNESDAY

5 THURSDAY

6 FRIDAY

7 SATURDAY

8 SUNDAY

MY SOCIAL LIFE

NOTES AND STUFF

....

....

....

....

....

SEPTEMBER 2019

S	M	T	W	T	F	S
1	2	3	4	5	6	7
8	9	10	11	12	13	14
15	16	17	18	19	20	21
22	23	24	25	26	27	28
29	30					

SEPTEMBER

	APPOINTMENTS/MISC	STUFF TO DO

9 MONDAY

10 TUESDAY

11 WEDNESDAY

12 THURSDAY

13 FRIDAY

14 SATURDAY

15 SUNDAY

NOTES AND STUFF

....

....

....

....

....

SEPTEMBER 2019
S M T W T F S
1 2 3 4 5 6 7
8 9 10 11 12 13 14
15 16 17 18 19 20 21
22 23 24 25 26 27 28
29 30

SEPTEMBER

16 MONDAY

17 TUESDAY

18 WEDNESDAY

19 THURSDAY

20 FRIDAY

21 SATURDAY

U.N. INTERNATIONAL DAY OF PEACE

22 SUNDAY

....

....

....

....

....

....

Taking a selfie at eye level

Taking a selfie at slightly above eye level

NOTES AND STUFF

....

....

....

....

....

....

....

....

....

....

....

....

....

....

....

SEPTEMBER 2019

S M T W T F S
1 2 3 4 5 6 7
8 9 10 11 12 13 14
15 16 17 18 19 20 21
22 23 24 25 26 27 28
29 30

SEPTEMBER

	APPOINTMENTS/MISC	STUFF TO DO
23 MONDAY		
24 TUESDAY		
25 WEDNESDAY		
26 THURSDAY		
27 FRIDAY		
28 SATURDAY		
29 SUNDAY		

NOTES AND STUFF

....
....
....
....
....
....
....

SEPTEMBER 2019
S M T W T F S
1 2 3 4 5 6 7
8 9 10 11 12 13 14
15 16 17 18 19 20 21
22 23 24 25 26 27 28
29 30

SEP-OCT

	APPOINTMENTS/MISC	STUFF TO DO
30 MONDAY		

ROSH HASHANAH*
QUEEN'S BIRTHDAY (AUSTRALIA – WA)

| **1** TUESDAY | | |

ROSH HASHANAH ENDS

2 WEDNESDAY

3 THURSDAY

4 FRIDAY

5 SATURDAY

6 SUNDAY

*Begins at sundown the previous day

ME + ME: A GREAT TIME!

Talking and singing to myself

BLAH BLAH BLAH

Arguing with myself

Fashion show with myself

Dancing with myself

NOTES AND STUFF

....
....
....
....
....
....
....

SEPTEMBER 2019

S	M	T	W	T	F	S
1	2	3	4	5	6	7
8	9	10	11	12	13	14
15	16	17	18	19	20	21
22	23	24	25	26	27	28
29	30					

OCTOBER 2019

S	M	T	W	T	F	S
		1	2	3	4	5
6	7	8	9	10	11	12
13	14	15	16	17	18	19
20	21	22	23	24	25	26
27	28	29	30	31		

OCTOBER

APPOINTMENTS/MISC

STUFF TO DO

7 MONDAY

LABOUR DAY (AUSTRALIA – ACT, SA, NSW)
QUEEN'S BIRTHDAY (AUSTRALIA – QLD)

8 TUESDAY

9 WEDNESDAY

YOM KIPPUR*

10 THURSDAY

11 FRIDAY

12 SATURDAY

13 SUNDAY

*Begins at sundown the previous day

NOTES AND STUFF

....

....

....

....

....

OCTOBER 2019

S	M	T	W	T	F	S
		1	2	3	4	5
6	7	8	9	10	11	12
13	14	15	16	17	18	19
20	21	22	23	24	25	26
27	28	29	30	31		

OCTOBER

APPOINTMENTS/MISC

STUFF TO DO

14 MONDAY

COLUMBUS DAY (USA)
THANKSGIVING (CANADA)

15 TUESDAY

16 WEDNESDAY

17 THURSDAY

18 FRIDAY

19 SATURDAY

20 SUNDAY

MY SOCIAL LIFE

....

....

....

....

....

....

NOTES AND STUFF

....

....

....

....

S M T W T F S
1 2 3 4 5
6 7 8 9 10 11 12
13 14 15 16 17 18 19
20 21 22 23 24 25 26
27 28 29 30 31

OCTOBER

APPOINTMENTS/MISC

STUFF TO DO

21 MONDAY

22 TUESDAY

23 WEDNESDAY

24 THURSDAY

UNITED NATIONS DAY

25 FRIDAY

26 SATURDAY

27 SUNDAY

MY SOCIAL LIFE

NOTES AND STUFF

....
....
....
....
....
....
....
....
....
....
....
....
....
....

OCTOBER 2019
S M T W T F S
         1 2 3 4 5
6 7 8 9 10 11 12
13 14 15 16 17 18 19
20 21 22 23 24 25 26
27 28 29 30 31

OCT-NOV

APPOINTMENTS/MISC

STUFF TO DO

28 MONDAY

LABOUR DAY (NZ)
BANK HOLIDAY (IRELAND)

29 TUESDAY

30 WEDNESDAY

31 THURSDAY

HALLOWEEN

1 FRIDAY

2 SATURDAY

3 SUNDAY

NOTES AND STUFF

....

....

....

....

....

....

....

....

OCTOBER 2019

S	M	T	W	T	F	S
		1	2	3	4	5
6	7	8	9	10	11	12
13	14	15	16	17	18	19
20	21	22	23	24	25	26
27	28	29	30	31		

NOVEMBER 2019

S	M	T	W	T	F	S
					1	2
3	4	5	6	7	8	9
10	11	12	13	14	15	16
17	18	19	20	21	22	23
24	25	26	27	28	29	30

NOVEMBER

APPOINTMENTS/MISC

STUFF TO DO

4 MONDAY

5 TUESDAY

ELECTION DAY (USA)

6 WEDNESDAY

7 THURSDAY

8 FRIDAY

9 SATURDAY

10 SUNDAY

MY SOCIAL LIFE

NOTES AND STUFF

....

....

....

NOVEMBER 2019
S M T W T F S
          1 2
3 4 5 6 7 8 9
10 11 12 13 14 15 16
17 18 19 20 21 22 23
24 25 26 27 28 29 30

NOVEMBER

APPOINTMENTS/MISC

STUFF TO DO

11 MONDAY

VETERANS' DAY (USA)
REMEMBRANCE DAY (CANADA, IRELAND, UK)

12 TUESDAY

13 WEDNESDAY

14 THURSDAY

15 FRIDAY

16 SATURDAY

17 SUNDAY

MY SOCIAL LIFE

PAST

PRESENT

NOTES AND STUFF

....

....

....

....

....

NOVEMBER 2019
S M T W T F S
                1 2
3 4 5 6 7 8 9
10 11 12 13 14 15 16
17 18 19 20 21 22 23
24 25 26 27 28 29 30

NOVEMBER

18 MONDAY

19 TUESDAY

20 WEDNESDAY

21 THURSDAY

22 FRIDAY

23 SATURDAY

24 SUNDAY

MY SOCIAL LIFE

Seeing a dog

Seeing a PUPPY

Seeing a PUPPY
in a SWEATER

NOTES AND STUFF

....
....
....
....
....
....

NOVEMBER 2019

S	M	T	W	T	F	S
					1	2
3	4	5	6	7	8	9
10	11	12	13	14	15	16
17	18	19	20	21	22	23
24	25	26	27	28	29	30

NOV-DEC

APPOINTMENTS/MISC

STUFF TO DO

25 MONDAY

26 TUESDAY

27 WEDNESDAY

28 THURSDAY

THANKSGIVING (USA)

29 FRIDAY

30 SATURDAY

ST. ANDREW'S DAY (UK)

1 SUNDAY

MY SOCIAL LIFE

NOTES AND STUFF

NOVEMBER 2019

S M T W T F S

          1 2
3 4 5 6 7 8 9
10 11 12 13 14 15 16
17 18 19 20 21 22 23
24 25 26 27 28 29 30

DECEMBER 2019

S M T W T F S

1 2 3 4 5 6 7
8 9 10 11 12 13 14
15 16 17 18 19 20 21
22 23 24 25 26 27 28
29 30 31

DECEMBER

	APPOINTMENTS/MISC	STUFF TO DO
2 MONDAY		
3 TUESDAY		
4 WEDNESDAY		
5 THURSDAY		
6 FRIDAY		
7 SATURDAY		
8 SUNDAY		

NOTES AND STUFF

....
....
....
....

DECEMBER 2019
S M T W T F S
1 2 3 4 5 6 7
8 9 10 11 12 13 14
15 16 17 18 19 20 21
22 23 24 25 26 27 28
29 30 31

DECEMBER

APPOINTMENTS/MISC

STUFF TO DO

9 MONDAY

10 TUESDAY

HUMAN RIGHTS DAY

11 WEDNESDAY

12 THURSDAY

13 FRIDAY

14 SATURDAY

15 SUNDAY

MY SOCIAL LIFE

FINALS SEASON

NOTES AND STUFF

....

....

....

....

....

DECEMBER 2019
S M T W T F S
1 2 3 4 5 6 7
8 9 10 11 12 13 14
15 16 17 18 19 20 21
22 23 24 25 26 27 28
29 30 31

DECEMBER

16 MONDAY

17 TUESDAY

18 WEDNESDAY

19 THURSDAY

20 FRIDAY

21 SATURDAY

22 SUNDAY

MY SOCIAL LIFE

NOTES AND STUFF

....

....

....

....

....

DECEMBER 2019
S M T W T F S
1 2 3 4 5 6 7
8 9 10 11 12 13 14
15 16 17 18 19 20 21
22 23 24 25 26 27 28
29 30 31

DECEMBER

APPOINTMENTS/MISC

STUFF TO DO

23 MONDAY

HANUKKAH*

24 TUESDAY

CHRISTMAS EVE

25 WEDNESDAY

CHRISTMAS DAY

26 THURSDAY

KWANZAA BEGINS (USA)
BOXING DAY (CANADA, NZ, UK, AUSTRALIA – EXCEPT SA)
ST. STEPHEN'S DAY (IRELAND)
PROCLAMATION DAY (AUSTRALIA – SA)

27 FRIDAY

28 SATURDAY

29 SUNDAY

*Begins at sundown the previous day

NOTES AND STUFF

....
....
....
....
....

DECEMBER 2019
S M T W T F S
1 2 3 4 5 6 7
8 9 10 11 12 13 14
15 16 17 18 19 20 21
22 23 24 25 26 27 28
29 30 31

DEC-JAN

APPOINTMENTS/MISC

STUFF TO DO

30 MONDAY

HANUKKAH ENDS

31 TUESDAY

1 WEDNESDAY

NEW YEAR'S DAY
KWANZAA ENDS (USA)

2 THURSDAY

NEW YEAR'S DAY (OBSERVED) (NZ)
BANK HOLIDAY (UK – SCOTLAND)

3 FRIDAY

4 SATURDAY

5 SUNDAY

MY SOCIAL LIFE

TAKING CARE OF...

My pets

Rub

My friends

My significant other

Myself

NOTES AND STUFF

....

....

....

....

....

....

....

DECEMBER 2019
S M T W T F S
1 2 3 4 5 6 7
8 9 10 11 12 13 14
15 16 17 18 19 20 21
22 23 24 25 26 27 28
29 30 31

JANUARY 2020
S M T W T F S
1 2 3 4
5 6 7 8 9 10 11
12 13 14 15 16 17 18
19 20 21 22 23 24 25
26 27 28 29 30 31

2020 PLANNING

JANUARY

_____
_____
_____
_____
_____
_____
_____
_____

FEBRUARY

_____
_____
_____
_____
_____
_____
_____
_____

MARCH

_____
_____
_____
_____
_____
_____
_____
_____

APRIL

_____
_____
_____
_____
_____
_____
_____
_____

MAY

_____
_____
_____
_____
_____
_____

JUNE

_____
_____
_____
_____
_____
_____

2020 PLANNING

JULY

_____
_____
_____
_____
_____
_____
_____

AUGUST

_____
_____
_____
_____
_____
_____
_____

SEPTEMBER

_____
_____
_____
_____
_____
_____
_____

OCTOBER

_____
_____
_____
_____
_____
_____
_____

NOVEMBER

_____
_____
_____
_____
_____
_____
_____

DECEMBER

_____
_____
_____
_____
_____
_____
_____

2018

JANUARY
S	M	T	W	T	F	S
	1	2	3	4	5	6
7	8	9	10	11	12	13
14	15	16	17	18	19	20
21	22	23	24	25	26	27
28	29	30	31			

FEBRUARY
S	M	T	W	T	F	S
				1	2	3
4	5	6	7	8	9	10
11	12	13	14	15	16	17
18	19	20	21	22	23	24
25	26	27	28			

MARCH
S	M	T	W	T	F	S
				1	2	3
4	5	6	7	8	9	10
11	12	13	14	15	16	17
18	19	20	21	22	23	24
25	26	27	28	29	30	31

APRIL
S	M	T	W	T	F	S
1	2	3	4	5	6	7
8	9	10	11	12	13	14
15	16	17	18	19	20	21
22	23	24	25	26	27	28
29	30					

MAY
S	M	T	W	T	F	S
		1	2	3	4	5
6	7	8	9	10	11	12
13	14	15	16	17	18	19
20	21	22	23	24	25	26
27	28	29	30	31		

JUNE
S	M	T	W	T	F	S
					1	2
3	4	5	6	7	8	9
10	11	12	13	14	15	16
17	18	19	20	21	22	23
24	25	26	27	28	29	30

JULY
S	M	T	W	T	F	S
1	2	3	4	5	6	7
8	9	10	11	12	13	14
15	16	17	18	19	20	21
22	23	24	25	26	27	28
29	30	31				

AUGUST
S	M	T	W	T	F	S
			1	2	3	4
5	6	7	8	9	10	11
12	13	14	15	16	17	18
19	20	21	22	23	24	25
26	27	28	29	30	31	

SEPTEMBER
S	M	T	W	T	F	S
						1
2	3	4	5	6	7	8
9	10	11	12	13	14	15
16	17	18	19	20	21	22
23	24	25	26	27	28	29
30						

OCTOBER
S	M	T	W	T	F	S
	1	2	3	4	5	6
7	8	9	10	11	12	13
14	15	16	17	18	19	20
21	22	23	24	25	26	27
28	29	30	31			

NOVEMBER
S	M	T	W	T	F	S
				1	2	3
4	5	6	7	8	9	10
11	12	13	14	15	16	17
18	19	20	21	22	23	24
25	26	27	28	29	30	

DECEMBER
S	M	T	W	T	F	S
						1
2	3	4	5	6	7	8
9	10	11	12	13	14	15
16	17	18	19	20	21	22
23	24	25	26	27	28	29
30	31					

2020

JANUARY

S	M	T	W	T	F	S
			1	2	3	4
5	6	7	8	9	10	11
12	13	14	15	16	17	18
19	20	21	22	23	24	25
26	27	28	29	30	31	

FEBRUARY

S	M	T	W	T	F	S
						1
2	3	4	5	6	7	8
9	10	11	12	13	14	15
16	17	18	19	20	21	22
23	24	25	26	27	28	29

MARCH

S	M	T	W	T	F	S
1	2	3	4	5	6	7
8	9	10	11	12	13	14
15	16	17	18	19	20	21
22	23	24	25	26	27	28
29	30	31				

APRIL

S	M	T	W	T	F	S
			1	2	3	4
5	6	7	8	9	10	11
12	13	14	15	16	17	18
19	20	21	22	23	24	25
26	27	28	29	30		

MAY

S	M	T	W	T	F	S
					1	2
3	4	5	6	7	8	9
10	11	12	13	14	15	16
17	18	19	20	21	22	23
24	25	26	27	28	29	30
31						

JUNE

S	M	T	W	T	F	S
	1	2	3	4	5	6
7	8	9	10	11	12	13
14	15	16	17	18	19	20
21	22	23	24	25	26	27
28	29	30				

JULY

S	M	T	W	T	F	S
			1	2	3	4
5	6	7	8	9	10	11
12	13	14	15	16	17	18
19	20	21	22	23	24	25
26	27	28	29	30	31	

AUGUST

S	M	T	W	T	F	S
						1
2	3	4	5	6	7	8
9	10	11	12	13	14	15
16	17	18	19	20	21	22
23	24	25	26	27	28	29
30	31					

SEPTEMBER

S	M	T	W	T	F	S
		1	2	3	4	5
6	7	8	9	10	11	12
13	14	15	16	17	18	19
20	21	22	23	24	25	26
27	28	29	30			

OCTOBER

S	M	T	W	T	F	S
				1	2	3
4	5	6	7	8	9	10
11	12	13	14	15	16	17
18	19	20	21	22	23	24
25	26	27	28	29	30	31

NOVEMBER

S	M	T	W	T	F	S
1	2	3	4	5	6	7
8	9	10	11	12	13	14
15	16	17	18	19	20	21
22	23	24	25	26	27	28
29	30					

DECEMBER

S	M	T	W	T	F	S
		1	2	3	4	5
6	7	8	9	10	11	12
13	14	15	16	17	18	19
20	21	22	23	24	25	26
27	28	29	30	31		

NOTES

GOALS

IDEAS

REMEMBER

THOUGHTS

DREAMS

CONTACTS

FAVORITES

STUFF

MEMORIES

_____
_____
_____
_____
_____
_____
_____
_____
_____
_____
_____
_____
_____
_____
_____
_____
_____
_____
_____
_____
_____
_____
_____
_____

MISC